Soaring Earth

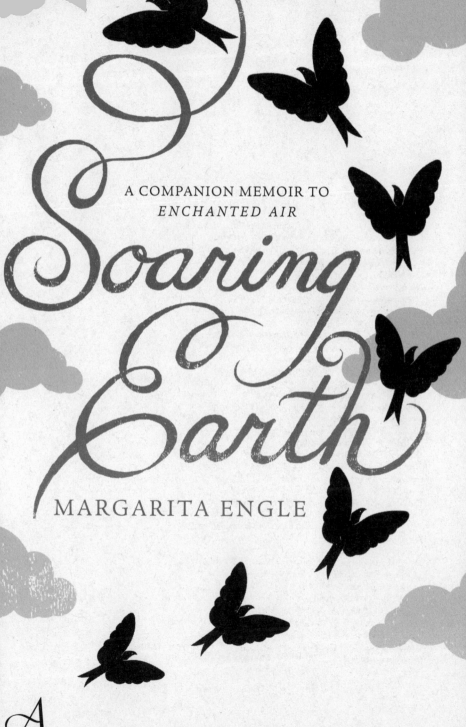

A COMPANION MEMOIR TO
ENCHANTED AIR

Soaring Earth

MARGARITA ENGLE

atheneum   New York London Toronto Sydney New Delhi

An imprint of Simon & Schuster Children's Publishing Division
1230 Avenue of the Americas, New York, New York 10020

For information about special discounts for bulk purchases,
please contact Simon & Schuster Special Sales at 1-866-506-1949
or business@simonandschuster.com.
The Simon & Schuster Speakers Bureau can bring authors to your live
event. For more information or to book an event, contact the Simon &
Schuster Speakers Bureau at 1-866-248-3049 or visit our website at
www.simonspeakers.com.
Also available in an Atheneum hardcover edition
Book design by Debra Sfetsios-Conover
The text for this book was set in ITC Legacy Serif Std.
Manufactured in the United States of America
First Atheneum paperback edition May 2020
10 9 8 7 6 5 4 3 2 1
The Library of Congress has cataloged the hardcover edition as follows:
Names: Engle, Margarita, author.
Title: Soaring earth : a companion memoir to Enchanted Air /
Margarita Engle.
Description: First edition. |
New York : Atheneum Books for Young Readers, [2019]
Identifiers: LCCN 2018003603 | ISBN 9781534429536
(hardcover : alk. paper) | ISBN 9781534429543 (pbk) |
ISBN 9781534429550 (eBook)
Subjects: LCSH: Engle, Margarita—Juvenile literature. |
Cuban Americans—Biography—Juvenile literature. | Women authors,
American—20th century—Biography—Juvenile literature.
Classification: LCC PS3555.N4254 Z46 2019 | DDC 811/.54 [B]—dc23
LC record available at https://lccn.loc.gov/2018003603

*for dreamers
whose dreams
seem impossible*

Soaring Earth

¡Volar sin alas donde todo es cielo!
Anota este jocundo
pensamiento: Parar, parar el mundo
entre las puntas de los pies,
y luego darle cuerda del revés
para verlo girar en el vacío . . .

To fly without wings where all is sky!
Note this cheerful
thought: To stop, to stop the world
between the tips of your feet,
and then spin it in reverse
to watch it twirl through space . . .

—Antonio Machado, "Poema 53"

❧ Contents ❧

EARTHBOUND

Summer visits to the enchanted air of Trinidad de Cuba are
illegal now, transforming my mother's hometown into
a mystery of impossibility, no longer reachable
in real life.

My roaming dreams can only ramble through the library,
dancing on flat, shiny pages, across all the countries of
National Geographic magazine, choosing villages
with brilliant sunlight, bright parrots, green jungles,
tropical heat.

I've endured enough of being in between—too young for
solitary trips, but more than old enough for motionless
teenage
isolation.

Yes, I feel ready to grow up and seize the first job that promises
a nomadic life . . .

but before I can finish college and become independent,
I have to start
high school.

Wide Air

1966–1968

TRAVEL DREAMS

Destinations sweep over me
from colors in dazzling photos,
a warm, inviting quality seen only in the light
of tropical air.

I'll save piles of babysitting money
and make my escape from Los Angeles.
No more smog, just a rain forest, peaceful
beneath sky so intense that each breath
must be enchanted like Cuba's *aire*,
floating birdlike and wild above jungles
and farms, green between two
shades of blue,
sea and heaven,
half wave-washed memory,
half soaring daydream.

Where should I travel?
Peru, Borneo, India?
The brightness of photos is dimmed
only by my age, too young for solitary
journeys, too old for imaginary
horse-friends.

REALITY

India sounds perfect,
but my travel dreams
have to wait.

High school starts right after
my fourteenth birthday, the halls
a
    whirlwind
of
    strangers . . .

but I'm pretty good at starting over
because I have plenty of practice saying goodbye
to the past, so after school, I sit on a rigid wall
wishing for the future, waiting to be older,
my current age a hybrid
half riddle,
half puzzle.

THE GEOGRAPHY OF A WALL

The wall is a barrier that separates
John Marshall High School from the street,
a dry imitation of my seawall memory,
that coral stone Malecón in Havana.

This wall is designed to separate waves of
raucous students
from dangerous riptides
of traffic.

Or is it just meant to keep rich kids and regular ones
apart? The wealthy have cars that zoom away
while the rest of us wait for a bus or a parent,
the wall dividing cascades of us into tide pools,
settled groups of relaxed kids who met in kindergarten,
and seaweed-like strays, those of us who transferred
from out of the district, and arrived knowing
no one.

Cool kids.
Loners.
Stoners.

Will I ever wash ashore in a swirling
puddle
of friendship?

With my wide Cuban hips
and frizzy black hair,
I'll never belong
with blond surfers
or elegant "socials,"
so I just have to hope
that sooner or later,
other drifting
bookworms
will find me.

ARMY M.

It doesn't take too many weeks on the wall
for one of the short-haired, military ROTC boys
to start flirting with me.

I'm Cuban American.
He's Mexican American.
Close enough.

But his army hair worries me.
How long will it be until he ends up in Vietnam,
killing
dying
or both?

I belong to a family of pacifists, always marching
to protest, because the Cold War has already sliced
our *familia* in half, so just imagine how much worse
it must be in southeast Asia, where US bombs
and chemical napalm flames
burn villagers alive
on the news
every night.

DATING

No war can last forever, so sooner or later
M.'s army world and my peace dove wishes
will surely meet in the middle.
Won't they?

Suddenly my plan to spend weekends babysitting
in order to save money for tropical expeditions
no longer seems as urgent as Friday nights
cruising around in a low-rider car,
my fourteen-year-old freshman mind
so imperfectly matched
with an almost-eighteen senior,
mi novio,
my boyfriend.

His older pals/*carnales* in the backseat
have already dropped out of school,
joined the army, fought in Vietnam,
and returned with tattoos
and all sorts of other
scars.

A WHIRLWIND OF MONTHS

Time
t
  w
    i
    s
t
s
and
   tangles,
spinning me
     far away
from unrealistic
       travel dreams.
Classwork.
Homework.
Research papers.
Friday nights cruising.
Saturday mornings at the Arroyo Seco Library
followed by babysitting jobs, my money stashed
and slowly growing toward some remote corner
of Bengal or Kashmir.

BOOKWORM

I can't stop, even though M.'s friends
make fun of me for studying hard
and reading travel tales in my spare time,
the places they've seen on their way to the war
so mysterious and adventurous to me,
a too-young girl who understands nothing
about battles.

Peace freak.
Flower child.
Hippie.

Army M.'s friends say it's easy to protest
against violence, when you're not the one
who will get arrested if you don't register
for the draft.

They're right—in wartime, life
is so much shorter for boys, since girls
aren't forced—or even allowed—to fight.

Bookworm. It's the creature name I've been called
all my life, but in Cuba
gusano/worm means maggot,
an insult used by revolutionaries for chasing away
anyone who wants to join relatives
exiled in the US.

Abuelita, my grandma,
is probably being mocked as a *gusana* right now
along with all the others who dream of fleeing
their wave-cradled isle and reaching
this hard, rocky shore.

Bookworm.
There are so many ways of looking
at the winged future of a crawling caterpillar.

But I'm finally identified and claimed
by an eager group of studious readers
who are mostly mixed-together half this,
half that, tolerant of everyone else,
hyphenated Americans, all our hyphens
equally
winged.
Japan, Korea, China, Poland, Holland,

Mexico, Cuba, the homelands
of our immigrant parents
don't really matter here
on the wall, where science
and poetry
are the passions
that unite us.

Some of my new friends have already
chosen career goals that require degrees
from the best Ivy League colleges,
so they load their after-school schedules
with extracurricular activities:
music, debate, theater, sports.

But the only club I would ever dare to hope for
is one made of girls who don't belong anywhere,
so a state university will have to be good enough,
with fancy-school admission reserved for others
who are courageous enough
. to perform
or compete.

DAYDREAMER

After those childhood summers in Cuba,
when my two-winged freedom to travel
was lost on both sides of the ocean,
I learned to imagine wholeness
by settling
into the weight
of motionless
earth.

But the world isn't heavy, not really,
it flies
through the galaxy
orbiting around the sun, spinning
on an invisible axis and soaring far away
all at the same time, while floating people pretend
that we feel safely
rooted.

So that's what I do, live two lives
awake and asleep, cruising or reading,
studying
dreaming . . .

I spend time with Army M.
and then my bookworm friends.
Night
and day.
I know how to balance

two spinning planets,
one in each hand,
like a juggler.
Don't I?

SPANISH CLASS

This quieter Mexican rhythm is natural
in a city where everyone says *mira*—look
instead of Cuba's *oye*—listen.

Perhaps this sense of language loss
is because our *familia* was so huge on the island
where relatives chattered, laughed, and shouted
at the same time, no one ever pausing
long enough to listen,
so that *¡oye!*
was the only way
to get anyone's
¡atención!

Now all those noisy, friendly cousins
might as well be living in another universe.
No travel, no summer visits, as if childhood
has been transformed into a fictional character's
imaginary wish.

When a Chinese American bookworm friend
who plans to be a Spanish teacher someday
accuses me of rolling my *rr*
in an exaggerated way
that's too long and trilling
like a cricket, I remember
how I was taught
by my *cubana* mother

who made me recite
over and over:
rr con rr guitarra
rr con rr barril
rápido corren
los carros
llevando las cañas
al ferrocarril.
Rr with *rr* guitar
rr with *rr* barrel
rapidly run the cars
carrying sugarcane
to the railroad.

Swiftly, with the rat-a-tat rhythm
of urgent island voices, that's the way
Mami said *rr* should always
race.

But I've been away from Cuba for so long
that my faith in what I know begins to fade
and I end up silently resentful, instead of
defending my own real
memories.

Will I forget Spanish
if I fail to travel
and practice?

Chichen Itzá en México,
Machu Picchu en el Perú.
Tikal en Guatemala.
Which ancient ruins
of magnificent cities
should I plan to visit
first?

MORE WHIRLWINDS

Wherever my mind wanders, history follows,
spinning and twirling—Vietnam War, Cold War,
military offense, self-defense,
Communist or anticommunist
conspiracy.

All these phrases I hear on the news every day
make me wonder why the US keeps trying to bully
this entire world, bombing countries
so far away.

My bookworm friends and I can't stop
those fierce overseas battles, so instead we protest
our school's dress code: let the boys grow long hair
and allow girls to wear jeans to class
instead of skirts.

We lose, of course, but at least we tried,
and the effort makes changing the spinning world's
direction
seem possible.
In the meantime, guys drop out of school
just so they can grow ponytails.

All the long-haired boys run away
to San Francisco.

Los Angeles begins to feel like a land
of abandoned girls.

It takes me a while to figure out
that the boys with shaggy heads
are imitating rock stars—the musicians
who mimic bearded revolutionaries
like my uncles and cousins
on the island.

For such a small place,
Cuba seems to have a way
of gripping the whole world's
atención.

TIME TRAVEL

At night, my mind spins
through flying dreams
as I rise and soar
superhero-style
arms reaching
forward
seeking
peace.

In dreams, I reject reality
and return to the blue-green-blue
isle of ocean-surrounded childhood,
a sliver of memory
treasured.

My only limitation is time.
Sooner or later, I'll have to wake up
and return to my motionless teenage self.

When I was younger, I imagined an invisible twin
left behind on the island, and now I wonder, was she
a dream, or is this sleeping self the real me?

IDENTITY

Even though I can't feel
like a real *cubanita* anymore,
I still fill my room with colors from the tropics,
a red piñata and a female canary, caged and songless
just like me.

In English class, I write a short story about Abuelita,
who was bold enough to be the first divorced woman
in Trinidad de Cuba, our town on the belly
of the long-lost, crocodile-shaped island.

My grandfather had epilepsy at a time when morphine
was the only cure. He tried Cantonese herbs,
Congolese *Santería*, and indigenous *curanderismo*,
but he ended up growing violent, and eventually
he died of an overdose.

The priest blamed divorce.
No wonder Mom still resents the Catholic Church.
She limits her faith to reading Quaker newsletters
that help weave the peace movement
deeply and firmly
inside my mind.

Dad says he's agnostic and also Jewish,
but he listens to a Hindu guru on the radio,
and when we go for a Sunday drive, he sits
beside a mountain stream and explains

that he's trying to communicate with nature
as he brushes swirls of watercolor
across a sheet of blank paper
that turns out to be
a magical sort of mirror
that can show peaceful trees
exactly the way they are
while leaving out man-made
roads and fences, returning
a patch of wounded forest
to its natural
wholeness.

Someday, maybe my poetry and stories
will learn how to alter language, creating
a timescape where past and future
can meet.

NOT LIKE ROMEO AND JULIET

When Army M. turns eighteen
I help his huge family throw a lively party
even though his tattooed buddies
make fun of me for wearing bell-bottom
hippie pants
instead of a shimmery
ruffled dress.

Army M. and I don't really break up.
He just leaves, and when he reaches
basic training, he sends me a photo
of his locker, with my school picture
taped up inside, smiling and wearing
sunflower yellow, a color that makes me look
like a stranger, because lately all I ever crave
is blue-green tie-dyed cloth, like Joan Baez,
the beautiful Mexican American Quaker,
a folk singer, my favorite poet
of peace.

SEPARATION

Branches
        of
                rivers
shift
        water
                rises
transformed into vapor
an airborne stream
of clouds
        and doubts.

                Alone in outer space?
Together on solid earth?
                No.
Just floating
                weightless
somewhere
                in between.

Without my first boyfriend
who am
I?

A QUIET HOME LIFE

No more Army M., just afternoons
cleaning a teacher's house, and Friday nights
babysitting to save for my mythical journey
to India, Borneo, or Peru, and then Saturdays
in the garden with Mom, planting trees,
hoeing weeds, bringing nearly dead plants
back from dry brown
into this soaring world's
memory
of green.

I live like an old woman, sewing and embroidering
while listening to Cuban music, smiling or crying
depending on the rhythm and how long it's been
since we received a letter from Abuelita
on the island.

How can a place remain so far away
while feeling as close as these blossoms
in my embroidered world
of silky threads?

COURAGE

My older sister works at the zoo, selling balloons.
Sometimes she walks into the wolf cage
as she studies to be a keeper.

On weekends, she wears a seven-foot
Colombian red-tailed boa constrictor
wrapped around her neck, the giant snake
that she bought as a pet and kept, even though
it keeps getting longer
and more powerful.

I'm not brave enough to do anything
but read
and daydream.

My only courage
is inside my secret world
of imagination.

BEST FRIENDS

Both of my closest bookworm friends
share the same name, so I think of them
as Short E. and Tall E., the first a delicate dancer,
the second happily rugged, wearing men's shirts
and helping her father invent laser light shows
that flash to the rhythm of rock music.

With Short E. I hitchhike, with Tall E. I hike.
Either way, we never really reach a destination,
just roaming like adventurers, exploring
the city or mountains.

But when Short E. starts smoking pot, her mind
slides away, first slowly, then swiftly, until she sees
people who aren't there, and hears threatening noises
beyond silent windows. . . .

Most of my bookworm friends are marijuana smokers,
but only Short E. suffers in this panic-twirled way,
yielding to nightmarish terrors while wide awake.

The sweet-scented leaves just make me feel dull and sleepy,
as I watch Short E. teeter at the edge of a cliff called
schizophrenia.

But we don't drift apart yet
not even when she thinks

she's a prowling cat
meowing.

Her long years of hospitalization
will come later.

For now, we are still both confident
that drug-riding minds can always
return.

BROTHERHOOD CAMP

Quakers love inviting everyone to meet,
get to know one another, talk, listen, or sit silently,
waiting for friendship.

I'm shy, but when Mom signs me up for camp,
I venture into the mountains with teens from all over
the enormous Los Angeles area, our neighborhoods
so far apart that we know we'll never
see one another again, and yet it feels right,
like a way of belonging to the whole world
all at once.

When a boy from Watts kisses me, we both agree
that if we lived closer, we'd get to know each other
at a normal speed, instead of so
briefly.

BOY CRAZY

I long to fall in love, believe in love,
convince myself that I'm capable
of love.

But back at school after Brotherhood Camp,
my next boyfriend zooms away on a motorcycle
to visit his Filipino family in a distant state.
I argue with my parents, begging to go with him,
but they shout no, and when he doesn't return
I'm almost relieved, because motorcycles
scare me, and courage is just something
I pretend
to understand.

Still boy crazy, I start dating someone else
almost right away, a polite and studious bookworm
who takes me to botanic gardens and an aviary
where a hummingbird lands on my curly hair
as if I've been transformed into a nest.

But this isn't love, it can never work out,
because the boy is friendly with my parents,
but he warns me that I'll never
meet his family.

They're from China, and he tells me
they would definitely think I'm too
foreign.

GLOBAL

In between real-boy craziness
and daydreams of imaginary guys,
there are books.

I'm shocked when the reading list
for world literature class is limited to Europe,
so I dare to read the *Mahabharata* from India,
Octavio Paz from Mexico, and anonymous
ancient poems from Japan, claiming my right
to explore
the whole globe.

When I turn in reports on books
from my own independent reading list,
the teacher is surprised, but she agrees
that it makes sense, and she accepts
my suggestions, even though they're
outlaws from beyond
the small-minded curriculum.

Sometimes all you have to do is wish
out loud.

HONORS CREATIVE WRITING CLASS

It sounds so exciting on paper
but the reality is frightening,
a critique group of teens
from all over the city
who sit in a circle
taking turns
smirking
as they tell one another
how much they hate
every poem
and each fragment
of a story.

So I stop writing. I freeze.
Strangers are impossible to please.
If I ever scribble again, I'll keep
every treasured word
secret.

SCIENCE

Without poetry, I can still love nature,
but the biology teacher is a sports coach
who mostly talks about the size of his wife's butt,
just to make the popular boys laugh.

So I sign up for a human physiology class
taught by a marine biologist who takes us
to tide pools and shows us the similarities
between octopus anatomy and humans.

All creatures are related, even odd-shaped
sea cucumbers, spiny urchins, and waving
anemones, with plantlike tentacles.

Back in our classroom, the teacher jumps
from the top of one wooden desk to another,
towering above us as she demonstrates
how a nerve impulse leaps across a synapse,
the microscopic gap between separate cells.
Crossing a chasm, that's what she says we need,
like a leap
                    of courageous   faith.

AIRMAIL

Letters to and from Cuba
arrive slowly, through a complex maze of other
countries, because nations that don't have
diplomatic relations
never sit together
listening
to each other.

Maybe there should be a Brotherhood Camp
for grown-ups—politicians and diplomats
all swimming and hiking, before singing
around a campfire, developing friendships,
or even kissing.

Whenever a letter from Abuelita
does manage to reach us, bright postage stamps
are paper-thin proof that the island
of my childhood
still exists.

WOMEN'S LIBERATION

Feminism is all over the news, and now
it's somehow entered our own home.
Mom goes out and finds a paying job
for the first time since she was fourteen,
when she had to drop out after eighth grade,
because Abuelita couldn't afford to send
two children
to school,
so only *tío* Pepe
was able to study,
while Mom—because she
was a girl—had to make money
by painting designs on ceramics,
while she waited to be old enough
for marriage.

Now that she's working in a store, I have to do
a lot more cooking and cleaning, but the effort
is worthwhile, because my mother finally feels
like her brother's
equal.

FREE SPEECH

I decide that I'll never get married.
All I want to do is travel and learn.
All I need is books, not boyfriends.

Most of the time, Short E. is fine, her mind
only slipping away when she's stoned.

Together we find rides all the way to Berkeley
to visit the university campus
where everyone shouts all the time, demanding
the right
to be heard.

War, racism, sexism, all the topics of the free-speech movement
are so important, but later, back at home,
I'm shocked when Mom
speaks aloud about Cuba at a Quaker meeting, and suddenly
she has to be escorted through the parking lot,
where anti-peace picketers see her as a target
for their hatred.

Free speech can be
so dangerous.

PICTURE DAY

I ditch school,
hiding in the park.

It will be a relief
to open the yearbook
and see
my absence
from predictions
that divide and compare girls—
cutest, coolest, most likely to succeed
as a movie star.

Someday when all of us are old,
this yearbook will prove that I really was
invisible.

WALKING TREES

I've read about a forest in Ecuador
where stilt roots grow at angles
that help trees aim themselves
toward patches of sunlight
by moving
    just a few
        inches
            per day
                until
                    the forest
                        has slowly
                            reached a new
                                home.

But I'm not patient, so I aim myself
toward Berkeley, expecting college
and the free-speech movement
to lead me directly to a rebellious
form of peace.

In April, when Martin Luther King is assassinated,
furious protests follow news of his death
all over this
    fractured
        country
so that riots result
even though King preached nonviolence

in a time   when the   vast   chasm

between war hawks   and peace doves
racists   and justice seekers
grows   grows   grows
wide
wider
wild.

Wild Air

1968–1969

COLLEGE AT LAST

The University of California, Berkeley,
my seventeenth birthday, I arrive alone
too stubborn to let my parents help me move
so far away
from
home.

Freak-out, uptight, laid-back, groovy,
bummer means bad news, and bread
means money.

I quickly learn the language of cool
rebellious youth, even though I also
suddenly feel
isolated
ancient
lonely.

Home is now a bed and a desk
in a cooperative dorm, where I work
in the kitchen, peeling potatoes to pay
for room and board.

One of the other girls is only seventeen too,
constantly sobbing for the four-year-old son
she was forced to give up
for adoption.

When we speak to each other, all our words
revolve like moons around the planet
of her spinning, agonized, orbiting
maternal
sorrow.

I'm no help at all.
What do I know of babies?
Years of weekends spent tending them
in exchange for bits of money
taught me nothing more
than how much simpler
life will be
if I never
fall in love
get married
give birth
care.

BRAIN WAVES

My parents are helping
pay for college, but I need a job,
and babysitting no longer seems
like the only choice.

So I soon find work as a test subject
in a psychology lab where grad students
attach eerie wires
to electrodes
on my forehead.

I look like a science-fiction book cover.
Weird gadgets record my hidden brain's
mysteriously pulsing reactions
as I watch funny movies
followed
by horrifying
war news.

If only politicians could see these results.
Maybe they'd decide to conquer the world
with comedy, instead of weapons.

CHOOSING MY FUTURE

With work and housing settled,
I need classes.

The world seems infinite.
So many choices!
Where do I start?

First I tour the museum-like halls
of science departments,
paleontology and anthropology,
the dusty bones
of dinosaurs
and cavemen
looming
like spooky
campfire tales, as if the past
might spring to life, clearly viewed,
a visual
prehistory.

Still undecided, I stand in one line
after another, hour after hour,
along with thousands
of other perplexed freshmen,
everyone complaining
that it's too much
too big

so many classes
are already full.

In the end, I find that I've registered
for Introduction to Physical Anthropology,
Italian Renaissance Literature,
Elementary Hindi-Urdu,
and Freshman Composition,
a class about writing essays
designed to convince me that I know
how to express my opinions.

The simple versions of Freshman Comp
were full, so the section I'm in is called
Rhetoric.

Am I really enrolled in a class about
arguing?

SURROUNDED BY STRANGERS

All the students at the off-campus dorm
are pre-med, pre-law, nursing, education,
black and white East Coast kids,
no one familiar, not even one person
from Los Angeles, or one who speaks
Spanish.

It's hard to explain why I want to study
an outdoor ology that will take me exploring
in distant tropical rain forests,
instead of a practical, profitable,
ordinary
urban career.

So I don't try to make sense of anything.

I just let myself be a stranger.

Childhood travels back and forth to Cuba
are kept secret, even from myself, because by now
I'm an expert in the slow-motion art
of forgetting.

THE STRANGENESS OF DAILY LIFE

The co-op dorm is on an avenue
crowded with shaggy panhandlers
who beg for spare change
while saffron-robed dancers
spin in circles, pretending to be spiritual
and Indian, even though they're just
middle-class white kids
having an adventure
as they beg too.

Homeless.
Hungry.
Stoned.
Drunk.
Street people wander
into the cafeteria
to seize food.

Some of them just eat and leave,
but others stay and talk, trying to sound
like students, fibbing about their identities
just so they can gobble the bland potatoes I peeled.
I don't care when they steal food,
but I'm wary. . . .

Some of these street people
seem gentle, but others are aggressive,

moving like boxers, always ready
to fight. . . .

Is my dream of peace
just an illusion
left over
from childhood?

ATTACKED

I'm in the hallway
headed toward my room.

A man in a suit follows me
from the cafeteria.

He's not a student,
he doesn't belong here.

I've always expected to die young
in this life where whole islands
can vanish.

So is this the moment when I'll be knifed
or shot?

Instead of a gun or blade,
he wields a long black umbrella,
knocks me down, pretends to stabs me
with the sharp handle,
then leaves me unharmed
but fearful, like a bird
stunned by flying
into a window.

DAMAGED

Only
my
confidence
in
the
world's
generosity
was
injured.

No scars.
Just an absence of belief
in kindness.

SEEKING A REFUGE

When another homeless guy walks in
and slaps me across the face, I know
that I need to stay away from the dorm.

This must be how girls
in Vietnam feel, with soldiers
charging
from the south
and north.

So I take my homework to the library,
where I spend most days and evenings,
only venturing back to the so-called
cooperative
at night
to sleep,
immersed
in a tsunami
of nightmares.

HOMEWORK

I love the huge library, with so many
quiet places where I can practice
writing phrases in Hindi, trying to master
all the dots, lines, and curlicues of Devanagari,
an alphabet shared by more than one hundred
languages.
Forty-seven letters.
Fourteen vowels.
Thirty-three consonants.
Everything dangles delicately,
like twining
vines
with shy
tendrils
that grow below lines
on the paper, instead of perching
above. . . .

The beauty
and complexity
of an unfamiliar alphabet
is a challenge,
but writing flows more freely
than pronunciation, especially
the nasal *eh* sound as I complete
my first sentence:
Mera naam Margarita hai.
My name is Margarita.

Aap ka kya naam hai?
What is your name?

Santre bahut ashe hai.
The oranges are very good—

Practicing feels as graceful
and challenging
as poetry.

I need to blow my breath into every hidden *h*,
watch the placement
of my tongue
against teeth,
control the shape of lips, until my mouth
is exhausted, then try again, persisting, never, never
giving up.

IS SEVENTEEN THE AGE OF WISHES?

Survival.
Love.
Travel.
So many dreams!
So little experience.

The only thing I really learned in high school
was how to learn.
Listen.
Wonder.
Imagine.
Dare to tackle difficult challenges.
Never expect to offer answers,
unless I'm sure I understand
the questions.

When all else fails, trust the library.
But this building at UC Berkeley is so vast
that I don't know where to start searching
for maps and guidebooks to help me choose
future destinations.
What about Cuba?

Will a return
to my mother's
homeland
ever

be
possible?

I would trade
decades of adulthood
for one more thrilling journey
to the lost
island
of childhood.

OVERDOSE

There's a guy in the co-op
who always seems happy.

I'm not sure what he's studying,
but when he invites me to a poetry reading,
I begin to wonder if we might turn out to be
more than friends.

Then he shows me his source
of so-called joy.
Pills.
He's miserable.
He takes me to hear B. B. King sing the blues
and to watch Jimi Hendrix smash a fancy guitar
against speakers, while sparks of raging music
flare.

Pills make their way
around the concert hall,
passed from hand to hand,
my chilling memory of Short E.'s
hallucinations
making me careful
to swallow
only one
tiny
tablet.

But my date takes too many,
and soon
he's on his way
to the emergency room,
his sanity   slipping   wandering   so far
that for days, everyone in the cafeteria
at the co-op
speaks of him
as if he might
never return,
and they're right.

One more   mind   lost
                    over that steep
                            cliff:
                            LSD
                            acid.

STILLNESS

I need to recover
from the shock
of a friend's
overdose
outdoors.

Nature.
The redwood forest.
No people, just trees,
this height
of sky . . .

and internal
size
of silence.

THE MYSTERY OF MOVEMENT

Back to classrooms.
Obediently seated.
Trying to listen.
Struggling to learn.

Opening library books.
Nothing is constant.
Everything changes.
Earth rotates at 1,000 miles per hour,
orbits the sun at 67,000 mph,
a total of 1,600,000 miles per day,
while the solar system glides 1,300,000 mph
within the Milky Way.

So while I'm seated, I'm really traveling
32,000,000 miles each day.

How many other illusions do I experience,
along with this one that fools me into thinking
I'm capable of choosing
my own
direction?

NO MORE BOYS

I'll never look at a guy again, not when there's
so great a chance that he'll die in Vietnam
or stay
and overdose.

HOMESICK HAIKU ON
A FOGGY BAY AREA DAY

I miss family
sunlight, smog, heat, friends,
and waiting to leave

REBEL T.

Tall, slim, friendly,
hair styled in a huge natural,
skin halfway between his light father
and dark mother.

He chooses to call himself only black
even though he's equally white,
just as I continue thinking of myself
as half-Cuban and half-American,
identity always such a personal blend
of inheritance
and surroundings.

But T. doesn't ask about my parents.
He assumes I'm Chicana, with ancestry
from Mexico, one of the four branches
of a growing movement at UC Berkeley—
the Third World Strike.

When Rebel T. asks me to join, I say yes,
and then we end up flirting, I'm not sure why
he chose me, when he's so bold, and I'm too shy.

PROTEST

We stand face-to-face
with policemen
in riot gear,
shouting
as we pretend
that we don't feel
any fear
of their helmets,
body armor,
gas masks,
weapons.

Our picket line looks like a war zone.
Maybe it is.
Third World means
neither capitalist nor communist,
but now it turns into a gathering
of young North Americans who feel left out
within US borders

Black, Chicano, Asian, Native American,
I don't fit any of the four categories
of ethnic studies classes demanded
by strikers, but I'd be eager to sign up
for any course that teaches forgotten history.

The only problem is that our strike is a boycott.
Standing face-to-face with the riot squad

means missing tests, so I'll flunk out
of Elementary Hindi-Urdu
Italian Renaissance Literature
Introduction to Physical Anthropology
and Freshman Comp/Rhetoric.

Devanagari is the skill I crave most.
Mastering a language requires daily practice.
Am I brave enough to sacrifice my only chance
to learn a second alphabet?
When I hold that calligraphy pen in my hand,
each foreign letter is a magical doorway,
inviting me to be pen pals with people
who live far away.

What do I crave more, rebellion
or communication?

SINGING MY OWN SECRET BLUES

I long to take midterms, finals,
and all the tests and quizzes
in between.

Yes, I need to pass all my classes,
stay in college, make any other sacrifice,
but not this one—not academic
failure.

If I tell Rebel T. the truth,
he'll think I'm a hypocrite, studying
India and Italy, instead of our shared
US.

THE TROUBLE WITH CHE GUEVARA

Rebel T., like every other non-*cubano* idealist
in Berkeley, keeps a poster of Che on his wall,
but Che wasn't just a handsome young wanderer
from Argentina; he was also a medical doctor
who joined my ancestral island's revolution
and then chose to kill people
instead of healing them.

He shot my relatives after they fought
with him
not against him.

So when Rebel T. asks about my *familia mexicana*,
I correct him—*cubana*, and he's instantly
so horrified
and outraged
that he calls me
una gusana.
He believes the myth
of a perfected revolution.
He assumes that I
am an enemy
of perfection.
He calls me a fanatic.
It's not true.
I'm not counterrevolutionary.
I just don't believe
in violence.

Gusana.

Maggot, not just worm.
Monstrous eater of dead flesh,
not a caterpillar waiting to be transformed.

From that moment on, Rebel T. refuses
to speak to me, except when he threatens
to kick me with his steel-toed boots
if I dare to cross his picket line
and return to my classes
in an effort to pass
tests.

I don't tell him about my uncle,
because he wouldn't listen anyway,
but when *Tío* Pepe was a member of Cuba's Olympic
sharpshooting team, he had to practice with Che,
who was known to be a poor marksman.
Pepe had to pretend that his own skills
were inferior, just to make sure that he didn't
get punished.

So I feel loyal to my uncle,
not to young North Americans
who still cling to the fantasy
of a heroic Che.

FUGITIVE

The next time I see Rebel T.
he's a face on the TV screen,
wanted for hijacking
an airplane to Cuba.

Maybe I should have warned him
that he'll be arrested when he arrives
on my ancestral island.

He won't be a hero.
He won't find acceptance.

What will it take for people
to give up their illusions?

Old Americans assume the island is hell,
while young idealists imagine
paradise.

C

It's a grade I dread, almost worse
than a D or F, because it's proof
that for a short while, I chose
a handsome rebel
over the treasured
opportunity
to learn Hindi.

Now I wind my way
through hidden
pathways, approaching
the classroom
a back way,
using redwood groves
that feel like serenity gardens,
instead of going anywhere near
the powerful
picket line
that defeated me.

¡MATA LA CUCA!

I keep going to class each day,
and in the evenings I serve as a volunteer tutor
for migrant farmworker children
way out in the countryside,
my transportation a local teacher
who accepts me into his eager crew
of Chicano students, even though I admit
that I'm *cubana*,
not *mexicana*.

Todos somos primos, he says.
We're all cousins.

It's the first time I've found a way to belong
in Berkeley.

The children I tutor show me how to shout
¡Mata la cuca!
each time we take our shoes off to smash
cockroaches
that scurry up and down kitchen walls
beside the table
where we drink juice
and practice reading children's books
written
only in English.

Why aren't there any bilingual stories,
so this whole farmworker *familia*
could understand
our lesson?

When I say good night, the parents walk me
to their door, asking what the word "Cuba" means—
is it a place?

Una isla del Caribe, I answer, wishing
that my mother's Caribbean island hadn't vanished
from so many emotional
maps.

¡HUELGA!/STRIKE!

On weekends I join a caravan of students
carrying food to farmworkers south of Fresno
in the town of Delano, headquarters for strikers
led by César Chávez.

We sleep on the floor of a house where the rice,
beans, and vegetables we deliver are served
to thousands of *filipinos* and *mexicanos*
who can't afford to buy the produce
they plant and harvest.

Fair wages.
Rest breaks.
Water.
Bathrooms.
Safety, sanitation, dignity,
their demands seem so reasonable,
but the grape boycott has dragged on for years.

Peaceful protests are slow, but worthwhile.
I feel certain that Chávez will succeed
in this situation where violence
might fail.

By the time I return to campus
I've learned two real-life lessons:
patience
faith.

A REBELLION IN REVERSE

Instead of getting stoned
with new friends at the co-op,
I read Vine Deloria Jr.,
N. Scott Momaday,
V. S. Naipaul,
Mariano Azuela,
Piri Thomas,
Octavio Paz.

Am I the only hippie
who dreads the sliding-mind effect of drugs
and finds myself
feeling high
on the poetry
of Paz?

The first thing we do every morning
in Elementary Hindi-Urdu is prayer hands,
a greeting,
namaste,
peace.

READY TO LEARN

The anthropology professor is perched on a stage
speaking to five hundred freshmen, explaining
that the definition of human has changed
now that Jane Goodall has observed chimps
making tools.

Do I need to alter my own definition
of self?

Another strike is swallowing Berkeley now,
this one called People's Park, the attempt
to turn an empty lot into a public space,
instead of letting developers destroy
lovely green
weedy
wildflowers.

Tear gas pours down from helicopters.
Running far below, we all weep, everyone
caught in the deluge of eye-scorching
riot squad
poison.

DEFEATED

Yes, I'm ready to change my definition
of self.

No more student life, erupting
in violence.

WILDERNESS

Hastily, in the midst of People's Park riots,
I plan a way to escape from this chaos.

I don't have a backpack, so I wrap
a cheap army-surplus sleeping bag
around my shoulders, and wearing
sandals instead of boots, I find a ride
to mountain peaks called the Pinnacles.

No tent.
No knowledge.
Stretched out on wet earth, I shiver
while common northern California rain
turns into a rare event—snow.

Hunger.
Why didn't I bring food?
Forest peace by day, frozen fear
at night.

Fragments of conversation
with groups of hikers, strangers.

By the time I reach
the Tassajara Zen monastery
I'm so grateful
for one tiny cup of hot tea
offered by silent monks

that the meaning
of that common word—gratitude—
grows into something enormous
and marvelous.

EXIT INTERVIEW

The counselors don't seem to care
why I'm covered with poison oak
or why I'm dropping out of college,
but they're expected to ask, so I tell
the truth, my freshman experience
has been too frightening,
with nothing but threats,
insults,
riots.

I thought I was brave,
but I'm scared.

The panel of three counselors
all nod, shrug, grin, and agree, yeah,
lots of other freshmen are dropping out too.

They don't ask where I'll go
or what I'll do
to survive.

Drifting

1 9 6 9 – 1 9 7 0

ANONYMOUS

I've lost my identity
no longer a student
my face in the mirror
this dropout
a stranger.

India?
Borneo?
Peru?
Not enough money.

Home?
I no longer know
what to say
to my parents.

Move across the bay
into San Francisco?
Maybe.

ANY BREEZE

The future is a dry leaf
weightless and floating . . .

so I agree to the first offer that comes along
when another dropout, looking for a roommate,
invites me to join her.
Why not?

Her hair is ice-blond, her name Scandinavian,
her goal so simple: find an apartment, get jobs,
live like grown-ups.

A TANKA POEM MADE
OF STOLEN HOPE

bold B.
teaches me to shoplift
but I only
do it once, the guilt
so deep that I almost drown

THE JOB MARKET

Bold B. finds night work in a topless bar
while I keep applying
at the post office,
city offices,
library,
stores,
anywhere
with daylight hours that would end
before the depths of my sinking mind
turn dark.

SEEKER

I can't find work.
I'm penniless.
I can't pay my share of rent.
So we part ways, Bold B. hunting
for a rich man to marry, while I drift alone
toward Golden Gate Park, Oak Street,
Haight-Ashbury, where I move into a commune
of strangers who behave like a family,
brothers and sisters, not lovers—
sharing expenses, cooking, housework.

I'm glad to have my own corner
of the rickety old wooden house,
a quiet room with a window seat
beneath a strip of stained glass.

When I open the window, I hear neighbors
chanting Buddhist prayers, but when I try
to join in, I discover that my restless mind
wanders toward daydreams, unable to grasp
the peace
of meditation.

MOODY

At first I work as a street vendor
making tie-dyed dresses
to sell in the park.

But it's not enough—all we eat at the commune
is rice and beans, so I find a job as a nanny
for a chubby baby
whose cheerfulness
makes my gloominess
bloom.

Where does his mother go every day
when she leaves her fancy apartment
dressed like a professor, carrying
an elegant briefcase?

How much college would I need
to become
so confident?

WEAVING

I take a bus to a wool broker's warehouse,
where I buy an entire fleece, newly shorn
off the sheep, this odor of lanolin
pungent and ancient.

A ritual of cleansing
by boiling
must follow.

Then I learn how to dye clean strands
with onion skins, wildflowers, and cochineal
beetle shells.

It feels satisfying to straighten tangles by carding
with nails punched into a block of wood,
then spin the colored fibers into yarn
by twirling a dangling spindle.

Building a simple wooden loom isn't easy
and weaving blankets is even more difficult,
each failure a way
of daring myself
to try again and again
until I succeed in producing
a few crooked works
of woven art.

If I can't graduate from college
at least
I can return
to a time in history
when degrees
weren't needed
to make useful items
out of animal hair.

MY REAL SELF

In the commune, women end up doing all the work
while men recover from the trauma of having
fought in Vietnam.

Draft dodgers on their way to Canada visit too,
escaping the fate of serving as soldiers in a war
that strikes all of us
as unjust.

Adventurers, transcendentalists, magic realists,
as soon as I plunge into San Francisco's vast library,
I feel at home in stories from other lands
and distant times,
a world filled with pathways
made of traveling words
on smooth paper.

Am I only myself
between the pages
of strangers'
memories?

MOON LANDING

A Quaker I knew from high school,
always angry, his draft number looming,
conscientious objector status rejected
by the military
because he doesn't attend
Society of Friends meetings
and can't prove
he prays.

Together for a few months, and then
when we break up, he speaks of leaving the country
while I go on vacation with my parents and sister
at a cabin
beside a wild river
where we watch
an astronaut take
his famous step
for mankind
on a lunar
landscape
that looks
quite a bit less desolate
than news photos of war zones
down here on this wildly spinning,
orbiting, soaring, impossible-to-understand
earth.

Yes, space travel is a scientific marvel,
but I still believe that the miracle
we really need
is peace,
not just technological
progress.

MUSICAL MADNESS

Even before the moon landing,
I'd started hanging out at the Family Dog,
an old building at the beach
where Jefferson Airplane
sings about white rabbits,
volunteers, and somebody
to love.

Free concerts.
Loud protests.
Stoned friends.

College, travel, peace,
and all my other daydreams
are so far out of reach that with
my patched jeans and ramshackle heart,
once again I choose the wrong guy—
a wanderer, Romany, with no plans
to stay.

Together, we roam out into the countryside
toward the green hills of Altamont
where the Rolling Stones are about
to perform "(I Can't Get No) Satisfaction,"
a song I danced to all the way
through high school. . . .

but the promise of music
is quickly ruined
by Hells Angels, the notorious
motorcycle gang
of tattooed men, who perch
on top of a truck
and hurl full beer cans at my head,
their drunken aim
the only thing that saves me
from a concussion
or death.

VIOLENCE

Knives flash.
A man dies.
Murder
instead of
music.

When I witness a killing
in those beautiful green hills
it makes me feel like no place
will ever be safe.

Never again will I hear a Rolling Stones song
without remembering fear
and sadness.

VOLUNTEER

Sober in a commune
of stoned friends,
I walk across
the tranquil park's
narrow panhandle
to a house with phones
where people take turns
answering questions
about hopelessness.

I never would have guessed
that I—who can't even begin to see myself
as an optimist—could end up feeling useful
as part of a suicide prevention hotline,
offering lists of reasons
to live.

THE HOUSE OF QUESTIONS

All sorts of strangers pass through the place
where I volunteer.

Researchers come around
offering doughnuts and hot chocolate
in exchange for answers about why
hippies drop out of college.

I answer in exchange for free food,
and even though the sociologists promise
to locate me again in thirty years, just to find out
how I turned out,
I know
they won't.

By then, they'll have moved on to other
more urgent subjects, studying teenagers
of the future, the children of people
who survive.

This country is so violent.
Surely I'll die young.

THE HOUSE OF SURPRISES

Volunteering for a hotline is tricky.
Some of the questions are unanswerable.

One day there's a girl who shows up
on the doorstep, crying because she misses Cuba
even though she's not *una cubana*.

Venceremos, she explains—We will win.
It's the name of a sugarcane-chopping brigade
for young foreigners who want to help the island's
revolution.

The girl says she just returned, and wants to go back
and stay forever, but the Cubans won't let her,
because they think North Americans need to stay home
and face our own problems.

So much time has passed
since I spent childhood summers with my relatives
that I've almost forgotten how desperately
I used to dream of living
on the island.

REMEMBERING MY OTHER SELF

Is she still there, my invisible twin,
the girl I would have been if we'd lived
on Mami's small, wave-tossed island
instead of Dad's
vast
rocky
continent?

WANDERING

I can't go back to Cuba
and I don't have money for India,
so I leave the city on a whim,
roaming north into comforting
redwood forests, where people
live in makeshift shelters—
water towers
tents
log cabins
on ranchlands. . . .

By the time I return to Haight-Ashbury,
babysitting, and my volunteer job
encouraging sorrowful strangers,
I feel capable
of wandering
anywhere.

ANOTHER STRANGER
AT THE HOUSE OF QUESTIONS

Is this love? Hate?
Foolishness?

Playing chess at one of the tables
in the house with the suicide hotline,
there's a bearded guy my age,
eighteen.

He's dressed like Che Guevara—dull olive-green
army fatigues.
I should be
suspicious.

He tells me I can join a Venceremos Brigade.
All I have to do is go to New York.
Sign some papers.
Escape.

I can't tell if he really knows how to help me
launch a journey all the way back to childhood,
but there aren't any legal ways
for US citizens
to reach Cuba.

The travel ban is specified
inside every American passport.

Not even those of us with relatives
on the isolated
island
are permitted
to visit.

ACTOR L.

My life seems to swirl in circles,
always returning to similar mistakes.

You don't need money, he promises,
just hitchhike to New York and join
the Venceremos Brigade there,
where everyone is signing up
to support one revolution
or another.

He claims he's an actor between roles,
a relative of famous Italian Americans,
movie producers, says he has Mafia connections, but
it's impossible to tell whether he's telling
the truth
or a story
from a film.

I should be
less trusting,
but I fill a knapsack
with camping food,
throw in a peasant blouse
and a skirt, ragged jeans,
and all the money
I've managed to save:
sixty dollars.

Abuelita,
my grandma.

Los tíos y primos,
uncles and cousins.

La finca,
the farm.

When I arrive on the island,
will anyone
recognize me?

CROSSING FROM COAST TO COAST

I can't be sure whether Actor L. is playing a role
or telling the truth, but I go with him anyway,
hitchhiking
thumbs up
begging for rides
in Nevada, Colorado,
endless desert, then mountain roads,
the soil changing color as we travel,
accepting the kindness of strangers.

I give the drivers gas money,
pay for their food, sleep in churches,
basically homeless, my throat on fire with strep,
this crazy adventure quickly changing into mere
survival.

By the time we reach Cleveland
I can barely sit up, and a few days later
I'm waiting in the emergency room
at Harlem General, surrounded
by men who bleed from stabbing
and gunshot wounds.

HOPELESS?

New York City terrifies me.
I should have stopped
in one of the farm states
and taken a job
milking cows
or hoeing weeds.

Skyscrapers horrify me.
Too much shade on the street.
Where's the sun?
Shrubs? Trees?

Homeless in Harlem?
My last twenty dollars
are stolen out of my bag
by someone seated next to me
in a church.

STREET PEOPLE

I'm one of them now
the drifters I used to fear
in Berkeley.

Once my money is gone
I'm no use to Actor L.,
but I run into him again
on the campus of Columbia University
where students are rioting, outraged
by the secretive US bombing of Cambodia.

With no place to sleep
I join a crowd of marchers
who seize an office in the administration building,
but I'm not willing to get arrested, so I find
a gentle Puerto Rican poet
who agrees to rent me a room
on credit.

Now I need a job—the Venceremos Brigade
will have to wait.

LOST

Discouraged.
   Dis-couraged.

Missing home.
Wishing
for
   a future.

Is bravery
   the same
as hope?

PAUSING TO SEARCH
FOR MY LOST SELF IN BOOKS

Once upon a time I believed
that poetry was a river where anyone
could swim, but fear of criticism
overwhelmed me, and now
all I have
is prose.

So I find the library
and read instead of writing.

Jorge Amado, Gabriel García Márquez.
In books, I find villages lost in time,
towns that remind me of Trinidad, Cuba.

When I discover that several
of my high school friends
have ended up all living together
in a rat-infested apartment
while they study at Columbia,
I visit, and they let me move in,
but as soon as he figures out
that I have help, Actor L.
shows up again, expecting shelter.

A junkie moves in with him,
both of them nodding off,
sleeping

the deep
indifference
of heroin.

Actor L. shaves his beard, then his head,
and joins some sort of militia
wearing a stern Maoist uniform
instead of his old Che Guevara costume.

Dis-couraged, I realize
that I'll never know
if he's simply acting
or really crazy,
maybe truly
dangerous.

UPROOTED

Without a college degree
I can't find a job anywhere
but I finally figure out how to apply
to the Venceremos Brigade.

They turn me away
simply because my mother
is Cuban.

Only North Americans with no relatives on the island
are allowed to chop sugarcane
swinging a machete.

My reason for hitchhiking
all the way to New York
has vanished.

Now, each time I step out
of the crowded apartment,
I have to dodge cat-size rats
that scavenge on the dimly lit
stairway.

SURVIVAL

Rent is due, but I'm penniless,
so I rush into any job I can find,
lasting only one hour
as a waitress.

When I lose my way
in the complicated subway system,
I'm chased by gangsters who threaten
to kill me, but then I'm rescued
by a young man
who leads me
from danger
to safety.

Even though he seems
like a dark-skinned, angelic
superhero, he's just a student,
the bravest
bookworm.

NIGHT SHIFT

The only work I can find
is plugging wires into a switchboard
as a telephone operator
in Greenwich Village,
trapped in a chair
until two o'clock each morning, when I ride
the dreary subway back to a crazy apartment
where Actor L. and his junkie friend
sit nodding off on the couch, while the bookworms
I knew so well in high school
study, study,
study. . . .

Will I ever manage
to return
to college?

Once an opportunity
has been abandoned,
can lost hope ever
be rediscovered?

USELESS

Seated at the switchboard, I learn
that I become numb in emergencies.

Each time someone calls for police,
ambulance, or fire assistance, my voice
falls silent, my hands tremble,
and I have to turn the urgent
cry for help
over to a manager.

I'm a coward, terrified of making errors.
It's the same fear that smothered
the breath
of poetry.

Why do I imagine
that in order to accomplish anything,
all my feeble, trial-and-error efforts
need to be
perfect?

WISHING FOR ENCOURAGEMENT

Encourage.
En-courage.
In courage.

When Actor L. threatens me
with a bone-handled hunting knife,
I toss it down the garbage chute,
but he comes back the next day
with an array of many blades,
all the shiny knives
perfectly
polished.

DISTANCE

During coffee breaks at work
I'm allowed
to make free long-distance phone calls.

I don't tell my mother about those sharp
cutting edges
that haunt my nightmares.

Instead we talk about family,
and she warns me to stay away
from Pepe, my uncle who is now
a refugee, settled in Elizabeth,
New Jersey, the second biggest
Little Havana
after Miami.

I didn't know he was here, so close,
just across the river from Manhattan.
A relative.
Someone loving.
His laughter.
A link
to the past . . .

but I've sacrificed my chance to belong
anywhere near him, because he can't risk
being associated with a Cuban American
foolish enough to try to volunteer

for the island's impossible
ten-million-ton
sugarcane
harvest goal.

Even though I didn't get to join
the Venceremos Brigade, I'm on record
as someone who tried to travel to the place
Tío Pepe
just escaped.

FACING REALITY

I know the truth about Actor L. now.
Crazed and dangerous, not just acting.

Barefoot and wearing a sheet, he treks
into Riverside Park late at night, performing
some sort of imaginary ceremony.

The line between militias and cults
is a fine one.

So I leave
on a road trip,
exploring
quietness.

IN THE LAND OF
TRANSCENDENTALISTS

Walden Pond, then Cape Cod,
this peaceful stillness
beside the wave-embraced rage
of an ocean.

I sleep on a sand dune
hushed
by the hum
and roar
of comforting
nature.

ORPHEUS

The story of an underworld journey
finally sends me back to that source
of discouragement—dropping out
of the university—but this time
I'll have to stay in my parents'
home
my old
room
four
walls
just
enough
space
to study.

I feel as if I've ventured too far
from the loves of my childhood,
nature
and poetry.

It's time to go back and try to find
courage.

Green Earth

1970–1971

AFTER THE DRIFTING YEARS

Back in Los Angeles
where I started—
no boyfriends
or daydreams
of pleasing guys
who only crave
complete
control.

I need
to rediscover
my original self
before I share real life
with anyone
else.

STARTING OVER

Living in my parents' house
is free, and boring jobs bring
enough money
for textbooks, while low
community college fees
make Berkeley's high tuition
seem like a wasted fortune.

File clerk at a travel agency.
Post office mail sorter.
Floater in a department store, moving
from department to department,
never knowing enough about anything
to answer a perplexed customer's questions.

I don't care if these jobs are dull,
just as long as my mind is free to travel
back and forth to science classes, learning
about nature's orbiting world,
all my wild movements
masked
by gravity.

MURDERERS

The south-central campus is so far
from my parents' northeast LA home
that I have to ride two buses each way,
one hour each, plus waiting for a transfer
downtown, right in front of the courthouse
where several Charles Manson girls stand
in a circle on the sidewalk, eerily
chanting.

The madman they worship
is on trial.
Some of the girls
will be convicted too.

I try not to stare, but our eyes meet,
and in that instant I know that I could have been
just like them, if I'd kept drifting, aimlessly
listening to Actor L. or any other dangerously
convincing
liar.

NOW I ONLY LISTEN TO PROFESSORS

Geology.
Geography.
Meteorology.
Botany.
The poetry of science
flows over me
like a waterfall,
flooding my emotions
with a sense
of belonging
on earth.

Rocks.
Continents.
Weather.
Plants.
My world is complete,
once I've learned
the rhythmic names
of human life's
neighbors.

GEOLOGY FIELD TRIP

The Grand Canyon.
Hiking.
Camping.
Scrambling
downward, through layers
of millennia, and then back up
to modern times,
stopping
at a cinder cone
on the way home,
one of those perfectly symmetrical
ancient volcanoes, way out in the desert
where silence, wind, and prayer
all feel like old
friends.

TUTORING

My new job on campus
is guiding welfare mothers
as they struggle to understand the difference
between natural minerals and man-made
concrete.

They tell me they've never left the city.
Geology is a subject they enrolled in
just to meet a requirement, but field trips
are too far-fetched. Who would tend
their babies?

So I sit in a room full of older women,
passing around samples of granite
as I point out the tiny, glittering,
nearly hidden crystals
of pink feldspar,
black hornblende,
smoky quartz.

Each time my home city of Los Angeles
erupts in riots, I'll remember these women
who grew up without any chance
to learn
how to distinguish
between rigid gray pavement
and the complex beauty
of nature.

I'll remember that they feel
such a deep sense
of belonging
nowhere.

GEOGRAPHIC LONELINESS

Sometimes an island-shaped emptiness
enters my veins and floats toward my brain,
surging like a storm tide that makes me wish
for Cuba.

Peace
between my parents' nations
seems impossible, so this yearning
is just as unrealistic as time travel
across all the light-years
of memory.

Do I still have an invisible twin
left behind on that lost *isla*, the farm girl
who knows how it feels to breathe
enchanted air
and ride horses?

METEOROLOGY

After I complete advanced geology,
physical geography, cultural geography,
and the baffling mystery of chemistry,
I study the science of weather, a field
so full of subtle air movements
that guessing is still acceptable
once all the charts and graphs
are cleverly sketched.

Storms mean a drop in barometric pressure,
the flow of hot and cool aerial currents
in not-quite-predictable patterns,
just like my future.

If I'd known how wide and wild my first
doomed attempt at college would be,
I might have started right here
in a smaller school, where none
of the professors have Nobel Prizes,
but oh, how they love
to teach!

THE CHEMISTRY OF A PEACEFUL MIND

Tests.
Terrifying.
Too sensitive.
Care too much.
Cry too easily.
Curl up inside, just like *el morivivi*,
the sensitive Mimosa plant
I remember from Cuba, with feathery
green leaves that snap shut
when touched,
then reopen
oh so slowly,
unable to trust.

Some of the guys I meet are attractive,
but there will be no more wildly drifting
boyfriends
for me.

BETWEEN CLASSES

Signs, posters, flyers against the war
and in support of the never-ending
farmworkers' struggle
for justice
along with a quest
for ethnic studies courses,
all the same hopeful
protests
as before.

LA RAZA

Todos somos primos. We are all cousins.
All Latinos are related—it's a phrase
used by a Chicano organizer
to let me know I'm welcome
at Mexican American protests
even though I'm *una cubana,*
too often stereotyped
as a worm,
la gusana.

The difference
between UC Berkeley
and LACC
is poverty.

Poor people don't care if I'm a bit different,
as long as we're united for the same
causes.

FAMILY LIFE

Short E. is still hospitalized,
and all my other high school friends
have moved away, chasing their own
college dreams, so yes, I'm lonely, but family
helps.

My parents have their own spinning worlds.
Mom works in a Japanese American dentist's office,
where she picks up fragments of the language,
just enough to tell patients when to spit
or rinse.

In her free time, she gardens, folds origami paper
into the shapes of flowers and animals,
or stitches quilts, creating northern warmth
in tropical colors.

Dad teaches art, paints on canvas,
and etches intricate scenes onto copper plates
so he can print them on paper, using a press
that looks medieval, the wheel he turns
as heavy as a planet, as he pushes ink
into the faces of Don Quixote
and the idealistic knight's loyal horse,
Rocinante.

When I visit my sister in Santa Barbara,
I discover that she still has her enormous

pet boa constrictor, and a fluffy dog,
a surfboard, a boyfriend. . . .

She works at a pie house
but never gets fat, and she lives
in a cottage by the sea, the same little house
where Aldous Huxley wrote *Island*, a novel
about a shipwrecked journalist
in a tropical paradise where people
try to prevent the sort of tyranny
found in *Brave New World*
and *1984*.

I envy my big sister.
Her life is active and friend-filled,
while mine is quiet, studious, book-wrapped,
just as it was when we were little, before
I began to explore
the meanings
of the phrases
"wide air"
and
"wild."

EARTHQUAKE!

The jolt is powerful,
a sideways shock followed by rolling
movements,
plates of rock
shifting
beneath the bed
where I lie
sleepless
praying
even though until now
I wasn't sure whether I would ever
really believe
in God.

PERPLEXITY

I understand the Richter scale
for measuring earthquakes,
and the classification of clouds
when discussing storm trends,
and I even know a bit
about predictions
of environmental disaster,
because I've read
The Population Bomb,
which shows
the overwhelming
mathematics
of future hunger. . . .

But I still don't understand
what to do with my life
until Introduction to Botany
changes
everything.

Somehow, confusion often leads
toward clarity.

GROWTH

Dr. H. stands in front of the botany lab
as we dissect potatoes.

Each "eye" is the bud of a stem
that can grow into an entirely new
separate plant.

You poor city kids,
Dr. H. says with a sigh,
you think strawberries sprout
from those little green boxes
at the supermarket.
Don't you?

She's right.
I've been away from Cuba's farms for so long
that I've forgotten about soil, roots, shoots,
flowers, fruit, and seeds.

Now I need to start over,
learning all that I knew so well
when I was little.

EVERY BREATH COMES
FROM SOMETHING GREEN

The poetry of botanical language
helps me feel hopeful.

Without plants, human life
is impossible—oxygen, not just food,
photosynthesis seems miraculous,
a magical transformation of sunlight,
the chemistry of molecules altered
by radiant rays.

In lab, we slice through plant organs,
then examine tissues under the lens
of a dissecting microscope
so that we can grasp
a clear view of membranes
and cell walls, all the places
where amazing reactions occur.

It's like peering into the not-so-distant past,
seeing a time when no human tribe survived
without understanding useful plants.

THE KINSHIP OF TREES

On walks around campus
there's taxonomy,
the relationships between species
found along pathways, all the trees,
shrubs, weeds, and flowering vines
equally fascinating—so many ways
to belong
on earth.

INSPIRATION

Dr. H. is Chinese American, her Japanese surname
the result of a marriage that enrages both their families.

She's a specialist in the tropical ferns of Costa Rica,
while he's a researcher studying magnetic fields
in Antarctica.

How easily my botany professor
defies
expectations!

She teaches me tidbits
of commonsense wisdom
that help me feel
prepared for life
on this planet,
as if I'm a creature
that has just arrived
from outer space.

Mangoes are related to poison oak,
so that's why the delicious fruit's peel
leaves a rash on my lips.

The sticky pollen of colorful blossoms
rarely causes hay fever, because those flowers
are pollinated by hummingbirds, butterflies, bees. . . .

Windborne pollen grains
are the real culprits,
rising from blooms
we barely notice,
the greenish flowers
of grasses and ragweed.

But the most important fact I absorb
during a thrilling series of botany lectures
is the history of agriculture, a skill invented
by women, while men were roaming
far and wide, hunting
or waging war.

Women and girls
were the creative gatherers
who harvested seeds,
then experimented
by planting.

Trying something new
came so naturally
to nomads who were always
hungry.

AN URGENT CAUSE

A green world.
Healthy seeds
in fertile soil.
Food for billions
of hungry strangers.
More and more billions
every few decades.

Desertification.
Trees are disappearing
dry regions spreading
geography changing
and once the trees
vanish
rainfall
decreases
the climate
is altered.

No way
to turn back.

I FIND MY FUTURE AT THE LIBRARY

Leafing through thick college catalogs
I choose a polytechnic university
and a major:
Agronomy.
Crop production.

This time, I won't give up.
I need to learn how to help feed the hungry
with roots, shoots, seeds, fruit,
and perseverance.

TRANSFER

The names of the classes
sound like a poem of plant growth—
vegetable production, irrigated pastures,
range management, weed identification,
cereal production, and just for fun—equitation,
riding horses!

But it won't be easy.
I'm one of the first two female
agronomy students
on this campus
and the only Latina.

I need student loans
and help from my parents,
as well as a job on the college farm crew,
hoeing weeds because the professors think
women shouldn't operate heavy equipment.

I can put up with their old-fashioned ideas
if it means having a chance to break
this glass ceiling.

POETRY REDISCOVERS ME

Once I know what I want to do with my life,
words, verses, and rhythms
return!

I start scribbling poems, and soon
I'm reading a slim bilingual volume
by Tomás Rivera—*Y no se lo tragó
la tierra/And the Earth
Did Not Swallow Him.*

I love the way verse and prose
Spanish and English
childhood
and growing
are all interwoven
in such a natural way.

Rivera's book is unique and familiar
at the same time, like an ocean wave
approaching from a distant island
where I existed long before I became
an adult.

Enchanted Earth

1973

PERSISTENCE

So much has changed.
Poetry miraculously returned
to my lonely soul, and sometimes
I'm almost
actually brave.

I've volunteered with a Quaker project
in an earthquake-ravaged village
on the high plateau of central Mexico.

I've wandered through Guatemala alone,
and joined a Sierra Club expedition
to study a wild mountain
in Montana.

I've spoken about farmworker rights
to a room full of the hostile sons
of farm owners.

Most of all, I've studied
and learned
without dropping out
when college life
grows confusing. . . .
And along the way
two separated halves
of my mind have floated
a little bit closer together

now that Abuelita, my grandma,
is a refugee in the US,
merciful asylum granted,
her Freedom Flight to Spain
just a detour on her way
to making our divided family
whole
again.

WHILE THE EARTH SPINS

Introduction to Arthropods.
It's a class about insects, spiders,
centipedes, millipedes, crustaceans,
and other invertebrates
with segmented bodies
and hard exoskeletons
outside their soft flesh
instead of within.

The eccentric professor
decides to experiment
by leaving the room
and instructing us
to figure things out
on our own.

Even though I've read the chapter
about insect mouth parts, I don't know
what to say in a small discussion group,
so instead
I listen
to travel stories
told by a handsome veteran
who was lucky enough to be stationed
in Oklahoma, instead of Vietnam.
He recently returned from a whole year
of wandering
all over the world,

from Portugal, Spain, and Morocco
to Turkey, Afghanistan, Pakistan,
India, Thailand, Singapore. . . .

A loyal dog named Flo
follows Curtis
from class to class.

I imagine that anyone
who is so patient and gentle
with a trusting animal
must be honest and kind
to people too.
I'm right.

EACH YEAR IS ONE SWIFT JOURNEY ALL THE WAY AROUND THE DISTANT SUN

Over the next few years
while we finish college
and graduate school,
we become best friends,
then eventually more. . . .

Our lives turn into
a love story.

Hope follows
wherever
we go.

AUTHOR'S NOTE

I never imagined there could be another time as turbulent as the 1960s. The Vietnam War, which seemed to last forever, should have served as a warning against the quagmires of twenty-first century, US-led conflicts in Iraq and Afghanistan. American high school students today have never known a single minute when their country was not at war. Peace, civil rights, freedom of expression, environmental causes, and all the other goals of my generation's protests are once again under threat. Defending those rights and freedoms is necessary, but protests sometimes grow violent, and when they do, it's confusing.

College is hard work, even in quieter times. Distractions and discouragement are common. Chaos and other challenges such as homesickness, hostile relationships, substance abuse, family pressures, or financial hardships can lead to dismay, even depression. More than half of all college students drop out.

Community college saved me. The classes were small enough for personal interaction with professors who loved to teach. Fees were low, giving me time to experiment by studying different subjects until I found one I truly loved. I wrote *Soaring Earth* because I hope that high school and middle school students who are already dreaming of college might realize that it's fine to follow any one of a variety of pathways. Big, famous campuses aren't the only ones that can offer an inspiring education. All that matters is choosing a place to start, and then persevering. I ended up working as an agronomist, botanist, and water conservation specialist, as well as a poet, novelist, and journalist. I have been married to the handsome guy with the dog for forty years, and I still feel like hope follows wherever love goes.

ACKNOWLEDGMENTS

I thank God for hope.

I'm grateful to Curtis, Flo, and the rest of our family for love.

For my thrilling role as the national 2017–2019 Young People's Poet Laureate, profound thanks to the Poetry Foundation. For ongoing encouragement, I'm grateful to Jennifer Crow, Kristene Scolefield, and the Arne Nixon Center for the Study of Children's Literature. For help with a phoenetic depiction of Hindi phrases, I am thankful to Gauri Manglik, Jaskaranjit Singh, and Kristi Miller. Thanks also to Mila Rianto, Sandra Ríos Balderrama, Angelica Carpenter, Joan Schoettler, and Ann Caruthers. As always, I'm deeply grateful to my agent, Michelle Humphrey, and to my editor, Reka Simonsen, and the entire publishing team at Atheneum.

Turn the page for a sneak peek of

With a Star in My Hand

ABANDONED

My first memory was one I could not understand
until years later: playing with towering animals
under a palm tree, all around me gentle eyes,
feathery green fronds,
and sticky tidbits of fruit
stuck to cow lips.

The cattle were smelly
and friendly,
just as hungry
for palm fruit
as I was
for milk.

Where did Mamá go?
I was too young for a sense of time,
but somehow I expected to be exiled forever
in that musical tangle of thumping hoofs
and clackety horns, my own wailing voice
adding a flutelike magic
to the noise.

LOST

When I remember abandonment,
all I feel is a sense of my smallness.

The roaming bulls ignored me.
I must have been too tiny
to seem
truly human.

Muddy legs, grubby face.
If I'd stayed in that cow world
long enough, I might have grown
hoofs, horns,
two more legs,
and a swishing tail.

WILD RHYMES

Jaguars, pumas, and other big cats,
poisonous snakes and vampire bats . . .

when Mamá abandoned me in a jungle,
did she think about all the fearful creatures
or was she merely offering me a green gift,
the sneaky hunt
for shy
sly
strangely
prowling
rhymes
to help me pass safely
through a dangerous
wilderness
called
time?

AM I AN ANIMAL YET?

With the rhythmic music of the herd
rattling through my busy mind,
I tried to moo like a cow,
coo like a dove,
then holler
and bellow,
just a lost and lonely little boy
whose human voice rose up
in an effort to transform
beastly
emotions.

No, I was not an animal,
but yes, I felt grateful
to four-legged creatures
for the lullabies they sang
to green trees
and blue sky.

Someday I will sing too,
instead of moaning.

FOUND

My mother's friend found me.
He was an angry farmer who spanked
my bottom.
Thwack!
Smack!
The crackling shuffle of rustling hoofs
sounded like a dance, as my cow friends
saw their chance to escape, leaving me alone
with the shouting stranger
who tossed me across
a mule's broad back,
where I bumped and swayed
all the way
to a palm-thatched hut . . .

but Mamá was not there
in the little house.
She had gone
    away.

LIKE A BIRD

Black eyes.
Slender hands.
Dark hair.
Waterfall laughter.

Trying to picture
my lost mother
has become a race
of entrancing words
that gallop
faster
and faster.

Did Mamá fly into the sky
like a winged being,
or is she alive
and hiding?

BIG MOUTH

A bearded man on a spirited horse
rescued me from the gloomy farmer.

We thundered far across the green hills
of Honduras, hoofbeats making me feel
like a centaur, as we galloped over the border
to Nicaragua—my homeland—but not
to the small room in the back of a store
in the little town of Metapa
where I was born.

Instead, we ended up in a rambling old
horseshoe-shaped house in the city of León,
where I was finally told that Mamá wanted me
to live HERE
with strangers.

I soon learned that the bearded rescuer
was my great-uncle, called El Bocón
by all who knew him.

Big Mouth, such a suitable nickname
for a man who tells tall tales
in a booming, larger-than-life
story voice.

He speaks of steep mountains with icy peaks,
and of gallant knights who battle ogres and dragons,
and of smoothly rolling hills in distant lands,
countries so remote
and amazing
that I can hardly absorb
the fascinating range
of exotic names.

Has he really traveled so much?
France? California?

Soon, when I grow up,
I plan to roam the earth
and be a Big Mouth too,
speaking truthfully
whenever I choose,
never caring
if anyone
is offended.

Any harsh fact is so much better
than telling lies like a tricky mother
who pretends
she'll just be gone
for a little while.